How to Write Your Life Story

How to Write Your Life Story

RALPH FLETCHER

Collins

An Imprint of HarperCollinsPublishers

Interview with Jack Gantos on pages 20–26 used by permission.

Interview with Jerry Spinelli on pages 57–61 used by permission.

Interview with Kathi Appelt on pages 86–95 used by permission.

Quotation on p. 52 is from *King of the Mild Frontier* by Chris Crutcher (New York: Greenwillow Books, 2003). Used by permission.

"Squished" on pp. 54–55 by Cyrene Wells is used by permission.

Collins is an imprint of HarperCollins Publishers.

How to Write Your Life Story

Text copyright © 2007 by Ralph Fletcher

Illustrations copyright © 2007 by Ian Nagy

Library of Congress Cataloging-in-Publication Data

Fletcher, Ralph J.

How to write your life story / Ralph Fletcher. — 1st ed.

p.   cm.

ISBN 978-0-06-050770-1 (trade bdg.)

ISBN 978-0-06-050769-5 (pbk. bdg.)

1. Autobiography—Authorship—Juvenile literature. I. Title.

CT25.F58 2007   2007010990

808'.06692—dc22

CIP

AC

Typography by Larissa Lawrynenko

1 2 3 4 5 6 7 8 9 10

First Edition

CONTENTS

The Buffalo

When I was little we called Dad's bathrobe his "buffalo." I don't know why we called it that, but we did. He traveled a lot during those years, selling textbooks to schools all over New England. When he came home Friday night, one of the first things he did was to put on that big, white terrycloth bathrobe along with his slippers. We would snuggle hard against his buffalo while he read stories to us before bed.

On Sunday night Dad loaded up his car and left to sell books. By midweek we would start pestering Mom. Could we get out Dad's buffalo? Just for a little while? She usually refused at first, but after a while she'd sigh and give in.

We'd race upstairs to the closet in Mom and Dad's bedroom. The buffalo always hung on a particular hook. We would jostle each other to be the first to pull it down and drag it downstairs to the living room. Then we'd wrap it around ourselves while we watched TV. The buffalo was big enough for two or even three kids to nestle inside its shaggy white bulk. Beyond its warmth and softness, the most wonderful thing about Dad's buffalo was how it had soaked up his essence, his *smell*. We would sit there, wrapped in the warmth and comforting scent of the father we missed so much. I discovered that if I closed my eyes and breathed in the smell, I could almost believe he was actually there, holding us in his strong arms.

Today the word *buffalo* makes me think of the mighty beasts that roamed the Great Plains until they were almost wiped out by hunters in the late 1800s. But for me the word has another, more personal meaning that's connected to my father. It reminds me of missing him all those nights when he was gone, plus the comfort and security I felt when he came back home.

Autobiography: Truths and Lies

I recently wrote a memoir titled *Marshfield Dreams: When I Was a Kid.* Working on that book taught me a great deal about pulling stories out of my life. In this book I'll share what I learned about autobiographical writing so you can write your own life story. Notice the last word of that sentence: *story.* It's not enough to merely put down information about your life; the trick is to fashion your memories into an engaging story.

What is a story, anyway? A good story should have three basic ingredients: characters (people/pets), setting (place/location), and plot (events/action). It helps to include some conflict, tension, trouble. It could include humor, a little romance, maybe even a few tears. All of it should be grounded in believable detail. Let's see if you have these elements in your life story.

CHARACTERS. You certainly have a main character that you know extremely well: you! You know that character's hopes, dreams, fears, and secrets. You also know the details of that character's life—that time in fourth grade when your mother bought a set of barbers' clippers and gave you a haircut that looked horrible. That was bad enough, but then you had to go to school and face your classmates. Other characters in your life story might include your parents, siblings, important relatives, friends, enemies, and teachers. And, yes, your pets.

SETTING. Your setting would include your neighborhood, house, and school. Settings can also include other places you have visited, like camp, places you went to on vacation, or your relatives' houses.

PLOT. Your story's plot is the action, the events that tell what happened in your life. You might write about the shock of moving from warm southern Florida to northern Minnesota, where winter temperatures hit thirty below zero. Or you could tell the story of how you found a stray dog who drove the family crazy at first but finally became its most beloved pet. There probably won't be one single plot, but a number of stories woven together to make up the fabric of your life.

As you can see, you definitely have the raw materials to write your story. In many ways, this is the easiest kind of writing imaginable. Think about it: You are the world's top expert on your life story. Nobody knows more about it than you do.

Why, then, do so many people get so bamboozled (one of my favorite words) and discouraged when they start writing their life story? I'm not completely sure, but I have some suspicions. I think too many people have been infected by the four deadly . . .

LIES ABOUT WRITING YOUR LIFE STORY

LIE #1: You have to be a famous celebrity.

Being as famous as J. K. Rowling or Tiger Woods might bring a multitude of readers who are eager to read juicy details about your life. But it's not necessary to be a rock star to write an auto-biography. In fact, many ordinary people have written the story of their lives. The trick is to write it in an honest, interesting way so that people will want to read it.

LIE #2: You must have an amazing life.

Have you overcome a terrible handicap, climbed Mount Everest, or spent a year living in the rain forest? Wonderful. Any one of these experiences will spice up the story you are trying to write. But chances are your life hasn't been quite as exciting as that. Mine sure hasn't. I grew up in a regular, run-of-the-mill house in a typical middle-class neighborhood in a sleepy Massachu-setts town.

Many people believe that you must have lived an amazing life to be a writer. I strongly disagree. In most cases, writers are people who simply find and tell the interesting stories in their ordinary lives. Often when we write about small, ordinary moments, we're surprised to find that other peo-ple, even total strangers, will relate to what we have written. Author Patricia Polacco remembered all the ways her big brother Richie use to torment her when she was growing up. Those memories became the basis of one of her most popular books, *My Rotten Redheaded Older Brother.*

LIE #3: You can't write your life story until you're old and gray.

Wrong! You've got something to say right now. All over the country, young writers exactly like you are writing powerful stories about their lives.

LIE #4: Nobody will read it, so what's the point?

Chances are pretty good that your immediate family—parents, older siblings, uncles and aunts, grandparents—will be interested in reading what you write. When you think of your audience, don't forget friends and teachers, too. And hold on to that story. Maybe your own kids will want to read it someday.

But the first and most important audience for your life story will be you. That's the way it should be. I'm betting that you'll enjoy writing it. You will learn a few surprising things about yourself in the process, and be proud of what you have accomplished when you see your story written down.

You may wonder about some of the words used to describe autobiographical writing: *Autobiography. Personal history. Memoir.* There are many different ways of writing about yourself, and in this book we'll explore autobiographical writing in all its variations. Most people will probably read this book from beginning to end, although I actually think it's impossible to digest any book about writing in one big swallow. A better way to read it might be to sample a bit, try some autobiographical writing of your own, and then come back to these pages for another nibble. But big bite or nibble, I trust you'll find a way to use this book that makes sense to you.

Let's begin!

Getting Started

So how do you get started writing your life story? You could simply begin with your birth: "I was born on October 31. . . ." and let the story find its own shape as you write. You could also kick off your story with an anecdote, an odd fact—even a joke.

But before you begin actually writing your story, it might be helpful to spend a few minutes digging up the raw stuff you'll need to make it interesting. Here are a few suggestions.

• **BRAINSTORM YOUR STORIES.** As I prepared to write *Marshfield Dreams*, I took out my writer's notebook and made a list of possible events, people, and things that might appear in my memoir. This list included:

1. *The War Against the Bees (my brother Tom)*
2. *The Screech Owl (my sister Elaine)*
3. *The Four Stooges (my best friends)*
4. *Smoking (both my parents)*
5. *Playing the Game of War (neighborhood kids)*

Eventually I had a list of thirty different items. This worked as a menu of ideas I could choose from when I wrote the actual book. I suggest you include everything you can think of when you make your list for the first time. When you reread the list, star or check the ones that seem strongest and most interesting.

• **COLLECT FAMILY STORIES.** Rita, my mother-in-law, always tells amazing family stories when we get together. One story involves the birth of her sister Mary.

"She was born premature," Rita explains. "She weighed only about a pound and a half at birth! She was so tiny, nobody expected her to live. After the doctor delivered the baby he told my mother: 'I'm sorry, but the baby probably won't live. I'll be back later with the death certificate.' My mother put Mary in a shoebox lined with cotton that was mixed with oil. The baby grew a little bit day by day. Amazingly, she survived!"

The story has been told many times. Even today it's one of the reasons that Mary is known in the family as a true survivor, someone who always perseveres through tough times.

In your family are there certain stories that get told again and again at holidays, weddings, reunions? Jot down a list of those stories, especially if one of them happens to involve you. It may be that you have only a sketch of the story. In that case, go back to the parent or relative who tells that story, and ask them questions.

How old were you when this happened? Did you see it?

What kind of oil did they put on the cotton? Baby oil? Mineral oil? Olive oil?

How did they feed such a tiny baby?

How did family members react to seeing the baby?

Getting answers to questions like these will give you the necessary details to flesh out the story so it will sound real and complete when you write it. Of course, any story is not a set of fixed facts.

It's a fluid narrative that will often differ depending on who tells it. Maybe you've noticed that your dad tells a family story one way, and his mom tells it differently. Ultimately, your job is not merely to recount these events but to create them, make them come alive.

• **GATHER ARTIFACTS FROM YOUR LIFE.** Get a box to gather things that have been important to you. These artifacts might include a beloved stuffed animal or doll, your first baseball glove, a scrap from your baby blanket, a photograph of you as the ringbearer/flower girl at a wedding, Girl or Boy Scout badges, old journals, or trading cards.

If you think about it, you'll realize that each of these objects is filled with memories. Hold the object, close your eyes, and see what rises into your memory. Where did you get it? Who gave it to you? Did it ever get lost? How did (does) it make you feel? When you start writing, having some physical artifacts on hand will help you ground your story.

• **WRITE ABOUT YOUR NAME.** This simple technique can help you unearth lots of great material for your life story. For example, I have written about the fact that my last name, Fletcher, means "arrow maker." In fact, the part of the arrow that has feathers is called the fletching.

You can do this as well. Ask yourself:

Who were you named after? Is there a story
connected to that?

What nicknames have you had?

Were you ever teased about your name?

Do people often misspell or mispronounce it?

How do you feel about your name?

Think about these questions for your first, middle, and last names and spend ten minutes writing about your name.

• **SKETCH A MAP OF YOUR NEIGHBORHOOD.** When I started working on *Marshfield Dreams*, one of the first things I did was to sketch a map of the neighborhood where I grew up. I closed my eyes and tried hard to picture that place as it once was—my house and yard, the bordering woods, the houses of my best friends Andy Hunt and Steve Fishman, a swamp in the woods, some wooden tripods we built in a clearing out back. Then I opened my eyes, took out a large piece of unlined paper, and started to draw.

As I did so, I discovered something surprising: The more I sketched, the more details I added, the more things I began to remember. As I made that neighborhood map, certain memories that I'd forgotten came back to me. You can see my map on pages 16–17.

I recommend that you try this yourself. The place you select to map out should be a place you know so well that you can picture it at night before you fall asleep—a neighborhood where you lived for several years, a relative's house or apartment you often visited, a vacation home, a summer camp you return to every year. You can even try it with the neighborhood you live in now. Don't try to make it look professional—just sketch what you remember, and make it as detailed as possible. As you do so, label your map to mark:

Where something happened (you lost a
    tooth, found a pocket knife, or buried a
    beloved pet)
A "power spot" (where all the neighborhood
    kids gathered)

A "danger spot" (a place you had to avoid)
A favorite place
A secret place

Instead of a treasure map, you are making a "story map," and it's very helpful. Many important stories are rooted in the important places in our lives. As writers, we get to dig those stories up.

• **MAKE A "HEART MAP."** I got this idea from Georgia Heard, a poet and teacher. A heart map is similar to a map of your neighborhood, with a twist—it's an emotional map of what matters to you. My heart map contains the things that are near and dear to my heart, such as my family, friends, nature, protecting the environment, the first amendment to the Constitution (freedom of speech), the Boston Red Sox, and dark chocolate! Page 19 shows a heart map created by Shamsun Nahar, a middle-school girl in Georgia. Note that some of the things she includes in the heart map are serious, while some are more playful (candy, deodorant). Shamsun also includes things (my future kids) she believes will become important in later years of her life.

A heart map is a great way to identify important things, people, events, and memories from your life. Try it yourself. Although the heart map deals with emotions, it doesn't have to be all serious. As a visiting author, I have worked with young writers across the United States. I met a boy named Terrence who made a heart map with a big section labeled "Circus Peanuts Candy." A girl named Olivia had a heart-shaped section in the very center of her map labeled "Ashton Kutcher," after the actor she's madly in love with.

Any of these strategies I've just discussed will help you dig up the raw clay for your life story. That's the beginning. Now you're ready to start thinking about how you'll mold that clay into the best story possible.

Interview with Jack Gantos

Author Jack Gantos has written books for little kids and big kids. His Rotten Ralph picture books have been read and loved by young readers all around the country. His three books about Joey Pigza, plus the Jack Henry stories, are perfect for middle-school readers. And he has written some terrific young adult books, including *Hole in My Life,* a memoir. *Joey Pigza Loses Control* was a Newbery Honor book.

Q: Could you talk about your writing process? How much prewriting do you do?

A: I'm not sure what you mean by prewriting. I write fiction, mostly, and so what I do is gather up key scenes and work at building bridges between them. I seldom outline, but I will make a quick list from time to time to organize the action and plot points. Once I gain the upper hand on the main portion of the story, I then do a lot of rewriting. It is in the rewriting that I refine the ideas, enrich the prose, shape and organize the action, and make certain that the story is crisp, clearly told, and paced in such a way that the reader has to read slow, rich prose when I want them to slow down and immerse themselves in the environment or setting. Then I write clean, direct prose when I want the reader to dash forward.

So for me, prewriting is synonymous with the moment of inspiration. If I had to fully outline every story before I wrote it, I would no longer enjoy the writing. There would be no risk in the creation, and without risk I would find little or even no passion in the work.

Q: When I wrote *Marshfield Dreams*, I started by making a map of my neighborhood. I know you do something similar with students when you make author visits. Can you talk about the importance of place in unearthing personal stories?

A: When I was a child I made maps of my neighborhoods not only so I could draw where "things happened," but also so I could capture them in my memory. We moved a lot, so a tangible map was helpful. Simply put, a lot of kids spend the majority of their time in their house, school, neighborhood, and sites where they have specific activities (sports, music lessons, theater, and so forth). The map has a way of concentrating in a small drawing a huge story. For instance, I have a map with a drawing of my dog and an alligator. From the drawing I can recall the entire story—what happened before the alligator spotted my dog, what happened when the alligator snatched my dog, and what happened after the dog was forever gone.

So the map is a way to find good material, and through the shorthand of drawing, to capture the essence of a story.

Q: How do you deal with writing about things you're not proud of—actions or events you might even be ashamed of?

A: For me, I go right at them. Ultimately, in art, the result is not shame, but the question is: Have I captured the shame with conviction and has the reader felt it deeply? I am not self-conscious about my questionable actions, but I am very sensitive to creating a story that is less than exactly what I want.

If you look at *Hole in My Life,* I dispense with the "crime" issue immediately so I can move on into the story, into the sweet spot of writing, which is not "what happened," but "how it happened."

Q: When you write a memoir how do you write the unpleasant truth about someone close to you (parent or sibling) when you know what you write might potentially hurt that person's feelings?

A: I seldom give this a second thought, though I do try to be fair. If I had to worry or guess at everyone else's delicate feelings, then I wouldn't write about them at all. If family members find a story about them unfair, then I challenge them to write a book the way they see it. Quite frankly, I find that most people are flattered to be the subject of a book, even if it is not flattering to their character. Yes, we all would love to be the morally correct, utterly handsome or beautiful, genius-level, clever-talking, brilliantly charming subject of a book—but the reader would be suspicious. I, for one, would gag if I read any account of myself that left out all my rotten qualities.

Q: What do you do when you're writing a memory but can't remember all of it? How much permission do you give yourself to "invent the truth"?

A: I can't remember every bit of dialogue from when I was eighteen or ten. But I can manage something that has the essence of truth to it. But I don't invent some fictitious parallel life and try to pass it off as memoir.

Q: Do you make discoveries when you write? When you wrote *Hole in My Life* did you learn anything about yourself that surprised you?

A: If you don't make discoveries when you write, there is no reason to write. Creation involves the unconscious mind, and as you write you give voice to thoughts and feelings that previously you had never defined. When I wrote *Hole in My Life* it was a surprise to take that material and carve it into words. Until then it had been more of an interior movie. Each moment was a surprise, not because I had never thought of it before, but because I had never knocked it into words before. And when I saw my life in an objective way—through the text—it seemed to be a very powerful foe. There was one Jack on paper, and there was another in my mind. Which one was going to be dominant? Which one was going to speak for me? Which one was more true? Well, these are big questions, and as any writer of memoir knows, there is a duality to the process that is inevitable. So which Jack wins? The memoir is one truth, and the memories are another. The reader will find truth in the memoir, and the writer will find truth in the memory.

The surprise is that they are both different and the same. A memoir is a very enigmatic form, and in writing one I have created my own double. This causes a great deal of conflict, because when I meet people who have read *Hole in My Life*, they are greeting the other me, the written me, and as I shake their hand I am aware that it is the flesh-and-blood me, the living me, doing the talking. It is as if I have become a hand puppet for the book.

Finding a Focus

If you're eleven years old you have already been alive for at least 4,017 days. Those days contain thousands of experiences, a jumble of friends and enemies, victories and defeats, praise and punishment, silly pranks and good deeds.

How can you possibly start writing when you've got so much stuff to choose from, so many days to write about? What you don't want to do is try to include everything. That would be too much material for any writer to juggle. And, honestly, an autobiography that tried to include every event from a person's life would be drop-dead boring.

As a writer you must be selective. With autobiography there's the promise made by the writer to the reader, unwritten but very real. The writer solemnly promises to omit as many dull, dreary, unimportant moments as possible.

It may be hard to leave out events from your life story, but it's necessary. As I mentioned earlier, when I wrote *Marshfield Dreams*, I began by listing stories, people, and events I wanted to include. But not everything on that list made it into the final version of the book. For example, I wrote one chapter called "Smoking." When I was a kid both of my parents smoked, as did most of the grown-ups I knew. Back then, people weren't as worried about being healthy, and smoking wasn't considered to be a bad thing the way it is today. During art class, we made papier-mâché ashtrays that we carefully painted, wrapped, and gave as gifts to our parents. In the Smoking chapter, I wrote that it's amazing how times have changed. My parents, like many other people, finally quit smoking. But in the end, the Smoking chapter didn't really go with the rest of the book. The other stories focused on the kids, not the grown-ups. Smoking didn't fit with those stories, so I left it out. It's not enough for each section you write to be interesting: You've got to make sure that it fits smoothly with the whole.

It may seem scary trying to tackle your whole life story. Don't be intimidated—see if you can find a smaller chunk to focus on. That chunk could be a particular story (the first time you rode a bike), or a person who strongly influenced your life (uncle, friend, cousin, rabbi, or minister). You might choose to focus on a particular place. When Jennifer wrote a memoir during sixth-grade English, she chose to focus on her camp:

Bye My Camp, I'll Never Forget You!

I'll never forget it. We actually sold our camp full of memories, love, fun, family. We actually sold our home away from home. There was no turning back. Our camp was no longer ours anymore. The word SOLD! was playing Ping-Pong in my head that whole day. Why did we have to sell it? That place is full of memories, that place IS a memory, a memory that is now walking in our footsteps, just pushed away behind us. No more Katie, no more

Meghan, no more Ben, no more concerts for the camp neighborhood, no more being stupid and riding a bike barefoot, no more boat rides in the shimmering sun, no more swimming in the cool, crisp water, and no more memories to write about—that is everything that went through my mind that day.

I will never forget you, my camp. You are truly a legend, a memory, and a friend in my life. I will never forget you.

Focusing on the sale of her family's camp allowed Katie to gather "snapshot memories" (*no more being stupid and riding a bike barefoot*). We can feel Katie's sadness as she makes an important transition from that carefree time in her life.

Finding a focus may come easily to you, or not. It may seem like you're starting with a hodgepodge of different ideas, all pulling you in different directions. If that's the case, look for a common thread. When Kat, a sixth grader, listed ideas for her autobiography, she noticed that many of the stories were connected to cooking—baking bread with her grandmother, helping her mother make soups and stews, cooking one night a week for her sisters when her parents had to work. Kat decided to title her autobiography "Cooking Up a Life." Now she had a title and a focus. Cooking provided the glue that would hold her story together. And brainstorming—her list of ideas—helped her find that focus.

I had a writing conference with Xander, a fifth grader. Earlier in the class his teacher had mentioned to me that this boy had been through a very hard time last year after his father died in a motorcycle accident. Xander showed me the map he had sketched of his neighborhood.

"Here's where me and my friends play baseball," he said, pointing. "And here's the playground. My grandfather gave me a cool watch, and I put it down over here, next to the swings, but then I went off to play. When I came back I couldn't find it. I once caught a foul ball off Derek Jeter, but I lost it over here, in these woods."

"Seems like you tend to lose lots of things," I said.

"Oh yeah! I had a pet turtle, and I let him walk

through the grass, over here, but he got lost and I never found him again. I'm always losing stuff!"

"You've lost some big things too," I pointed out. "Your teacher told me that you lost your father last year."

When I said that, Xander lowered his head. He nodded sadly. Xander ended up writing a memoir titled "Lost Along the Way." That main idea—loss—gave him a focus for his story.

Notice that both Kat and Xander used a title as a theme or main idea to help focus their stories. You might try this yourself by playing around with a possible title for your story. Write a few different versions of your title, and see if that helps you find your focus.

If a theme such as loss sounds too abstract, try something more concrete and physical. You may find that a physical object such as a toy, photo, memento, keepsake, or blue ribbon, may be just the thing to help you focus a slice of memoir, as I did with "The Buffalo" at the beginning of this book. Look at how Adam, a fourth grader, was able to use an old baseball glove as the seed for his memoir.

The Glove

Slowly, the catcher's mitt fell to the floor, along with dust, moths, and memories of baseball. The MacGregor with its golden brown leather lying limp on the floor, the red M staring up at me as if saying: "Try me on." Among the other gloves it was genuine with its knots knotted tight.

It was a day for baseball.

As I pulled on the thin leather over the top of my hand, I noticed a clammy, lost feeling to it. My dad had dreams of the major leagues, but he took a different path . . . family, instead of fame.

My dad explained the glove's past to me, and how he used it until he got out of college. He told of the sensational feeling of many watching eyes, contemplating your every move, wondering what you'll do next, envying your contribution to the team. Wondering what they <u>could</u> have accomplished if they went the extra mile.

The pop sound of the game is like a piece of thick plastic bending in half, stretching its limit, until ccrrreeeeeeekkk and a loud BAM! The crowd cheers with glee as the ball zings to your mitt at sixty to eighty miles per hour, the sting on your hand.

"What a good feeling that is," my dad exclaims.

"I bet it is," I answer.

It was a day for baseball.

I flip the glove like a dead fish, out of breath, my father's name faded upon the leather.

"The glove is so old," my dad says. "It's as old as me."

I laugh out loud as I ponder the thought of how my dad sort of abandoned the glove, and how the glove waits for a new owner.

"Why did you lock it away?" I ask him.

"What?" he says.

"Why did you lock it away in storage instead of keeping it out with the rest of your gloves?" I ask.

"Because I had no use for it, I don't play baseball anymore," he explains. "I'm an insurance agent, not a baseball player."

"But you could have used it for something else." I had recently been playing outfield, the most boring position on the whole field.

"Why are you asking me all those questions?" he loudly protests. "Why is it so important to you to keep it out?"

I don't know why, but somehow I feel better knowing that this glove will not go in storage for a long time. Then my dad remembers my question from before.

"You really want to play catcher?" he asks.

I nod.

"It's a lot of hard work," he points out.

"I'm ready," I announce.

"All right, then." He smiles.

Now, that clammy feeling no longer exists. It lingers with a sweaty-palm feeling and the smell of baseball.

Now I'm the catcher, not my dad.

It's uncanny the way physical artifacts seem to soak up our important memories and personal history. Look through your boxes, junk drawers, and old collections to see if you can find an object that feels like an important relic of your life. Hold it in your hand, close your eyes, and see what stories rise to the surface of your mind. Then write them down.

~~

Thinking About Form

This book is about writing a personal history. It's important that we all mean the same thing when we talk about various forms this kind of writing can take. Here are some brief definitions:

BIOGRAPHY—a nonfiction account of a person's life written, composed, or produced by another writer.

AUTOBIOGRAPHY—a nonfiction account of a person's life written by that actual person.

MEMOIR—a kind of autobiography in which the writer looks back on a certain time period, special relationship, or angle on his/her life. Looking back, or reflecting, is crucial to this kind of writing. The word *memoir* comes from the

French word *memoire,* which means "memory." Author Katherine Bomer says, "The memoirist takes a slice out of the pie of life and writes about it in a way that makes others care and want to read it." That's exactly what Xander did when he wrote "Lost Along the Way," mentioned in the last chapter.

What do you want your autobiographical writing to look like when you finish it? It's important to consider this question early in your process. One option is a traditional narrative: an introduction, various chapters about your life so far, usually in the order in which the events happened, and a proper ending. While that may be the way most folks shape their personal history, it's not necessarily the best one for every writer. In fact there's a whole smorgasbord of options available to anyone who creates a piece of autobiography or memoir. Here are four worth considering.

• **THE VIGNETTE OR "MICRO-MEMOIR."** Your autobiography or memoir doesn't need to be a hundred pages long. Sometimes a vignette, or a series of them, can be more effective than a long-winded story. The dictionary defines a vignette not as a story but as a "short, usually descriptive literary sketch." I think of the vignette as a "micro-memoir" because it can be quite short. Check out *The House on Mango Street* by Sandra Cisneros. This popular book contains many chapters about the most ordinary subjects: "Hairs," "My Name," and "Boys and Girls." Some of these chapters are barely one page long!

I wrote many short vignettes in *Marshfield Dreams*. The following chapter, "Junior," is a mere 123 words, less than one printed page:

Junior

As the oldest of nine, I was named after my father. and my grandfather. Some kids on Acorn Street teased me, calling, "Hey, Juuuu-nioooor!" Not that I minded. I liked having the same name as my father, but it did cause confusion in the house.

Whenever Mom called out, "Ralph!" Dad and I would both answer, "Yeah?"

"No, Big Ralph!" or, "Little Ralph!" she yelled back, to clarify things. I guess that would have *annoyed some people, but it didn't bother me. Dad was tall and handsome. I bragged to my friends that my father was so cool he had three jobs: teacher, milkman, and bartender. I was proud of him. I loved knowing that "Ralph" could fit us both in one snug syllable.*

As you can see, when you write a vignette you don't include everything. The challenge is to take one aspect of your life and select only what's essential when you describe it.

• **SNAPSHOTS.** A snapshot is even shorter than a vignette, often just a few sentences or one paragraph. Get your hands on *When I Was Young in the Mountains*, a picture book by Cynthia Rylant, illustrated by Diane Goode. Rylant's book isn't a typical story with a beginning, middle, and end. It's a series of small moments, or snapshots, capturing moments in time from the author's life when she was growing up in West Virginia.

Jenika Shannon, a student in Florida, read *When I Was Young in the Mountains*. She liked this book so much she decided to model her own writing after it:

When I Was Younger in West Tampa

When I was younger in West Tampa,
Ramen noodles were considered a "high-living"
    dinner.
Staying out at Grandma's was a vacation,
Even if it was just for six hours.

When I was younger in West Tampa,
A bicycle was just as good as a motor scooter.
A lunch box was deemed as a deep freezer,
Two cans of pop and a few bologna sandwiches,
No more than a meal for two could have been
    carried at once
Not that we had much anyway.

When I was younger in West Tampa,
What we had was abundant to me, but sparse to
    others,
The simple joy of prancing to the nearest super-
    market
Was my fantasy,
Working at the convenience store
My dream.

My problems were scarce,
My worries scant.
But then again, so was my joy.

Writing with snapshots is like spreading out a number of memories or "mental photographs," and then briefly describing each one. Notice that Jenika doesn't write a sequential story but a series of snapshots, using words to make the pictures of her life. I admire many things about this piece. Jenika includes several well-chosen details that vividly convey her life at that time in West Tampa. At the end she stands back, reflects, and makes a larger statement about her life.

Whether you use the vignette or the snapshot form, you'll want to think about some kind of "connective tissue" between the parts of each one, something to pull your stories together. In her memoir, Jenika borrows a technique used by Cynthia Rylant in *When I Was Young in the Mountains*: the recurring line. In *Marshfield Dreams*, I put a photograph of myself or my family at the beginning of each chapter. I thought that using photos like this would be a good way to connect all the chapters. It's a funny kind of balance—each vignette or snapshot should be able to stand on its own, but you also need to use something consistently to signal the reader that each story is part of the whole that is your life.

• **POETRY.** I can't think of any other genre that allows a writer to say so much with so few words. Poetry has a way of cutting through the fluff and getting down to what really matters. In the following autobiographical poem, Daylan Arean, a student from Florida, reveals a great deal about her life and how she has changed:

Where I'm From

I'm from a white, messy room,
With posters of squeaky boy bands,
To Tahitian candles
And collected blue walls
That smell like teen spirit.

I'm from six different homes,
Five different schools,
Three different dads,
And two different languages.

I'm from Ninja turtles
To the Iliad.
From Goodwill and Marshalls
To Gap and Tommy.

I'm from "Ewwww, cooties!"
To "I believe in dragons, decent men,
And other fantasy creatures."
I'm from wide-eyed and shy
To outgoing and cocky.

I'm from poverty and
Black beans and rice
To success and luxury,
And one-day dreams
I haven't even dreamed yet.

• **MULTI-GENRE.** One unique way of writing your life story is to put together a collection of very short pieces, each one a different kind of writing. You might pick from the following list, or come up with others on your own:

Letter

Interview

Interior monologue

Help Wanted advertisement

Weather report (describing yourself as a
     particular kind of weather)

Free-verse poem

Haiku

Acrostic poem

Personification poem: *I am a grassy field* . . .

TV commercial

Recipe

Personal ad

Prayer

Diary

Parody

Obituary

Music lyrics

If you're going to create a multi-genre autobiography, you won't use all these kinds of writing. Five or six different ones will probably be enough.

Multi-genre writing can be a lot of fun. It allows you to find playful, inventive ways to reveal different aspects of yourself and your life. Nicole, a fourth grader, wrote part of her autobiography as a Wanted notice:

WANTED

Nicole is wanted for having too many pets!

In total Nicole has 24 pets (when she is only allowed to have 16 pets)! You will find her mostly at Budget Pets and Petco. She will have lizards hanging from her ears and she will be wearing a blue shirt with dogs on it.

Reward: PET SERVICE FOR A MONTH.

As you can see, you've got several choices about what form to use for your autobiography. But writing your life history isn't like ordering a main course at a restaurant—you won't be stuck with your first choice of form. You might start writing your life story in one way, and then switch to another. The trick isn't necessarily to find the coolest, snazziest way. Rather, you want to find the form that feels best suited to the story you're trying to tell.

Crafting Your Story

This chapter deals with how to harness your powers as a writer to make your story come alive. Many books have been written about the writer's craft. In this chapter I've selected four craft tips that will be especially helpful with autobiographical writing.

• **WRITE SMALL.** I'm talking details here. Your life story will probably include some big issues, for example, battling an older kid who bullied you on the bus, the anticipation of a new school or new baby sister, or the move to a new home. To make those ideas come alive, you'll need to reveal them through specific details.

Let's say you write, "The day I moved to Ohio,

my best friend Greg gave me some weird stuff he collected." The curious reader will want to know what kind of stuff? That sentence comes alive if you tap into the power of the particular:

"The day I moved to Ohio, my best friend Greg gave me his prize collection of decapitated piñatas."

In *Marshfield Dreams* I described something that happened when I first started school. My younger brother Jimmy would find treasures in the woods and give them to me when I got off the bus.

> That afternoon when I got off the bus, Jimmy was at the bus stop, tapping his feet, eagerly waiting for me.
>
> "Look!" He had a small animal skull in his hands.
>
> "What is it?"
>
> "I think it's a beaver," he said. "Too big to be a cat. I found the bones in the woods. Here. It's for you."
>
> The next day when I stepped off the bus, he gave me an old wasp's nest. Every day, as soon as I got off the bus, he'd hand me a treasure he'd found in the woods.

You can see that the big ideas—Jimmy cared for me, and missed me terribly when I went to school—are fleshed out by the small details in this example of how Jimmy gave me those peculiar presents.

Here's a secret that may surprise you. *Marshfield Dreams* is a "true" memoir, but when I wrote it I made up certain details when I couldn't actually remember them. Honestly, I don't remember exactly what Jimmy gave me those first two times I got off the bus. I invented the two details—small animal skull and old wasp's nest—because those are exactly the kinds of things Jimmy would have found in the woods.

Of course, you shouldn't alter the main parts of your life story, adding a stepbrother if you didn't have one, or making your father a professional baseball player if, in fact, he was a plumber. But you can make up small particulars that you can't remember. If you stay true to the spirit of the book, and invent details that fit with the characters, they will sound convincing to a reader and will help your story come alive.

• **INVIGORATE YOUR VERBS.** Consider this sentence: *My hot, tired, sweaty feet dipped into the cool, sparkling, refreshing water.*

That's not an example of vivid writing. The sentence is terribly overwritten, in danger of collapsing from the weight of all those adjectives! Adding a ton of adjectives is like pouring too much syrup on a waffle. It won't make your writing strong.

I'll tell you a secret: It's not the adjectives or the adverbs that create vibrant writing. It's the verbs. Take a look at this paragraph:

> On August 19, at five A.M., my dad got me out of bed to go deep-sea fishing. I didn't want to go (I don't like anything nautical) but he asked me nonstop until finally I said okay. After all, it was his fiftieth birthday. The wind was making a small chop, and a series of small waves hit the bow of our boat as we went toward Georges Bank, where the big fish are.

Notice what happens to the writing in this paragraph when I upgrade the verbs.

On August 19, at five A.M., my dad <u>dragged</u> me out of bed to go deep-sea fishing. I didn't want to go (I <u>detest</u> anything nautical) but he <u>badgered</u> me nonstop until finally I <u>caved</u> in. After all, it was his fiftieth birthday. The wind had <u>kicked up</u> a small chop, and a series of small waves <u>spanked</u> the bow of our boat as we <u>steamed</u> toward Georges Bank, where the big fish <u>roam</u>.

You don't want to overdo it by adding a series of exotic, unusual verbs that call attention to themselves and send your readers heading for the dictionary to look them up. But be conscious of your verbs. The nouns create the pictures, but the verbs make those pictures move. Your writing will improve instantly if you find intriguing and muscular verbs to drive those sentences.

• **CREATE YOUR CHARACTERS.** The characters in your story may include parents, siblings, camp counselors, close friends, pets, and maybe even an enemy or two. If you want your story to engage readers, those characters must be interesting to read about.

When it comes to the characters in an autobiography, there's a built-in danger. Since these characters are familiar to you, you might get lazy and assume that your readers will automatically know them too. Don't! You can't just put your characters into your story and expect them to come alive in the mind of your readers. Instead, you must actively create them as you would fictional characters. The challenge is to reveal those characters not just on the outside, through their hair color, size, car, and clothes, but also through their inner lives—their hopes, fears, and flaws. Here are three tools for making your characters believable:

DIALOGUE

Mr. Waverly picked on certain kids, like Tommy Kimball, who always sat in class with his mouth partly open.

"If you don't close your mouth," Mr. Waverly told Tommy, "a fly will land in there."

GESTURE

Bryan viciously ripped off a chunk of bread, spraying crumbs everywhere.

TELLING DETAIL

Uncle Paul's idea of a perfect vacation was to

sleep until noon and stay in his pajamas all day long.

Let's see how a professional does it. In his autobiography, *King of the Mild Frontier*, Chris Crutcher wrote this description of a dangerous man named Ray:

> He was about six feet, five inches tall and weighed more than 300 pounds, almost always dressed in a cowboy outfit. It was not a Roy Rogers outfit, with which I may have been better equipped to identify from my youth, but a real cowboy outfit: boots and leather pants and a huge belt buckle with long cow horns above the caption YOU CAN HAVE MY COLT FORTY-FIVE WHEN YOU PRY IT FROM MY COLD DEAD FINGERS.

Notice that Chris Crutcher lists several details about Ray, but he saves the best one for last because he wants that one to have the biggest impact on the reader.

• **WAKE UP YOUR NARRATOR.** It's easy to forget that *you* are the most important character in your life history. You're the narrator, the one telling your story. Try to write the way you would speak. That way, the writing will sound like you. This is called *voice*. A strong, believable voice is the most essential ingredient when writing a personal history.

As the narrator, you'll be in the dual role of telling and reflecting, both of which are important. At the same time, it's essential for readers to see you *doing*—reacting to events, expressing emotion, interacting with other characters. You can't sleepwalk through the piece; you've got to be involved. When a memoir works well, the narrator is an active character, someone we feel we know from the inside out.

Here's part of a memoir written by a fifth grader named Julia.

> Do you know how a heart sounds? Well, if not, labump! labump! labump! That's what a healthy heart is supposed to sound like, and I should know because I had one, at least I thought I did, until my mom took me to the doctor's office for my three-year-old checkup. Then Dr. Wells put his stethoscope to my bare chest and heard something he

shouldn't have heard, something that would change the next two years of my life. . . .

The following piece was written by Cyrene Wells, a teacher and writer. In this "memoir patch," the author shares an event from her childhood. The piece has strong voice and a nice balance of external actions and inner feelings.

Squished

I hadn't played in our old sandbox for a long time, and grasslike weeds were growing in the hard sand. There wasn't much to do, and I was pretty bored.

A toad came around the edge of the sandbox near my feet. I watched as it stopped moving and sat still, facing away from me. It didn't move for the longest time, and after a while I reached across the sand for a stick to poke at it. When I poked him in the back he moved forward but not very much. I poked again, and he moved forward a body's length. I poked again and again, nudging him, and it seemed to irritate him. He was hopping this way

and that way like he really wanted to go somewhere but didn't know which way to go.

After a while I wanted to see how high he'd
jump, so I poked him lightly on top of his body.
Nice hop. I poked some more, becoming less gen-
tle as I did. Finally I poked straight down on the
toad (not even hard), and his guts came out of his
mouth—easy like toothpaste out of a tube.

First I dropped the stick. I thought about the
trouble I'd be in if anyone found out what I'd done.
So, I dug a hole in the sand and got a piece of bark
to scrape up the deflated toad and then his
insides. I lifted them to the hole and dropped them
in. Then I covered everything over—feeling sick the
whole time.

Every night when I went to bed I prayed hard
because I figured that squishing the guts out of a
toad was something I could go to hell for. About a
week later I got a wart on my finger. I couldn't fig-
ure out if the wart was punishment God had sent
so I wouldn't have to go to hell—or if the wart was
a sign that God had seen what I'd done and would
take care of me later. I never got the nerve to tell
the priest at confession what I'd done.

The power of Cyrene's piece comes partly from the fact that she's telling a secret, something she's not the least bit proud of. Cyrene includes details that give us a vivid (almost TOO vivid!) picture of this incident with the toad. I was struck by the balance of the "outside story" (what she does) and the "inside story" (how she feels). The voice of the narrator is strikingly honest, which gives the writing its power. Even if we don't approve of what she did, we trust that she's telling the truth. Writing with real honesty isn't easy, but it's a crucial element of strong autobiographical writing.

Interview with Jerry Spinelli

Jerry Spinelli has written many award-winning books, such as *Maniac MacGee, Stargirl,* and *Wringer.* He has also written a terrific memoir, *Knots in My Yo-Yo String: The Autobiography of a Kid.* I asked him to share a few insights about how he wrote *Knots in My Yo-Yo String.*

Q: I like your map at the beginning . . . especially the legend. Could you say more about the map— why you included it? Did making that map help you generate ideas to write about?

A: I guess the map emphasizes that this book is exactly what the subtitle says: *The Autobiography of a Kid,* emphasis on *kid.* It outlines the parameters of this kid's "world" while the legend notes milestones and features that distinquish the geography of this particular kid from all others.

Q: What planning or digging up did you do before actually beginning to write your memoir?

A: That's one of the things that made this book maybe my easiest to write. For starters, I didn't have to cook up a plot. The plot in this case was simply my life; all I had to do was remember it—and tap the memories of others, such as my mother and brother and some friends. And it was fun paging through all those old family albums and scrapbooks. And those ninth-grade love notes from Judy Pierson. I took the precaution of getting her permission before releasing them to the world. (She had her reservations at first; now she's happy because "You made me a star!")

Q: Did you rely on pure recollection when writing these memories? Were there any places where you allowed yourself to embellish/create any small details that you couldn't remember?

A: Yes, I'm sure I embellished here and there, to clarify and complete a picture for the reader, not to change the substance of what happened.

Q: You write about how you heard Virginia Cory sing off-key, and how you felt embarrassed for her. Was this hard to write? Is it hard to say a not-so-nice thing about a real person?

A: Well, yes, it's hard to say a not-so-nice thing about a real person, and I've left many items out of many books because of this consideration. As for Virginia Cory, honestly, I guess I felt that after fifty-five years she wasn't going to be hurt by a little thing like this—in the unlikely event that she ever reads it in the first place. She was a nice, friendly girl and a pal of mine; I know she wouldn't hold it against me. And note the last paragraph of that section; that's the whole point, how her song and my experience of it ultimately became a benchmark of my maturity. She may have been off-key, but she was a winner—a point I expanded into a book with *Loser*.

Q: The central metaphor of your book (knots in the yo-yo string) pulls the book together. You tried to attain perfection, but couldn't quite pull it off. How did you come up with that? Did you start with the image or did it evolve as you wrote the book?

A: The title came last. I hate that. When you're having a title problem like that, one thing you can do is go back into the text and see if your title is in there somewhere waiting for you. That's what I did, and there it was. So it was not so much a matter of designing the book around the title as distilling the title from the brew.

Q: Did you learn anything about yourself in the process of writing *Knots*? Did anything surprise you?

A: I guess the thing that surprised me was that I enjoyed the whole process more than I expected to. Originally I had been asked by a publisher to write my autobiography—which is the only way I would have written it. I would not have presumed on my own that anyone would care to read a book about me. As it was, I hesitated for quite a while before finally agreeing to do it. No sooner did I sign the contract than I regretted it. I just didn't feel comfortable featuring my own self in a book; it felt like inviting myself to the prom. But now I was committed, so I began talking to my mother and brother about the old days, and I returned to Norristown and walked along the old railroad tracks, and soon, in spite of myself, I was having something pretty close to fun.

The "So What?" Question

One night in mid-December I was having dinner with my family.

"On TV they were showing some kids in Montgomery, Alabama, making snowmen," I announced.

My sons Robert and Joseph exchanged puzzled looks.

"That's pretty . . . random, Dad!" Joseph said. "So what?"

"It hardly ever snows in Montgomery, Alabama," I explained. "Those kids probably haven't seen any snow in three years."

"Oh," Joseph said, understanding.

This conversation shines light on autobiography, and how it differs from regular old story writing. You know that a personal narrative is a story about something that happened to you. Most readers will understand that you wrote about getting stuck in a thunderstorm with your grandmother, for instance, because (1) it's an unusual event that happened, and (2) it makes a pretty interesting story.

With memoir or autobiography, however, it's not enough just to tell a good story. With this kind of writing readers will wonder, Why did the writer include this? What's the point? When you're writing your life story, readers expect that you communicate *why* this event is important, what it says about you as a person and your life as a whole.

The fancy four-syllable word for this is *significance*. In strong autobiographical writing, the author reflects on why the subject (person, place, or event) is significant—why it matters, what it means to the author. You do this by showing through examples, telling through reflection. Here's an example.

One day my father bought me a brand-new mountain bike, a blue Scorpion 360. The next day he told me we were going to move to California for his new job. After that I always had a funny feeling about that blue Scorpion. I hardly ever rode it. I always wondered: Was that mountain bike some kind of bribe to make me accept the idea of moving?

Adults have the luxury of looking back at events that happened years ago. The passage of time can help you get perspective. As you can see from "The Buffalo," I felt bad that my father traveled so much and worked so hard when I was a child. Often he was gone from Sunday night until Friday night, and I missed him. Now, as an adult, I realize how much my father was a product of history. He was born in 1929, the year the stock market crashed and when the Great Depression began, during which many people lost their jobs. Men born in that time grew up in a world where earning a steady income was valued above spending time with their children. Now that I'm older, and a father myself, I understand this better. I still remember what it felt like to miss my father, but the years have given me more perspective about why he worked so much.

When I wrote *Marshfield Dreams* I had never before written a memoir. I had to learn by doing it. Luckily, I had a good editor, Christy Ottaviano, who made a very useful suggestion.

"Look at the way you end your chapters," Christy said. "In some cases you don't go quite far enough. You might consider adding a few sentences, or a paragraph, to show the reader what this event means to you, and why it's important."

I had written one chapter, "Bobby," about one of my brothers, who would later get killed in a car accident. The chapter ended with me lifting Bobby, when he was a baby, out of his playpen. Christy suggested I add a sentence or two at the very end. Here's the chapter in the published book; I've underlined the lines I added at the end.

Bobby

Bobby was baby number five. He sat in the playpen happy as pie like he had no idea what was coming, which of course he didn't. How could he? How could any of us? Bobby seemed no differ-ent from the rest of us—he ate, slept, played, argued, laughed, watched TV, took baths, rode the school bus, complained about having to go to church. But he wasn't like the rest of us. Bobby never got the chance to grow up. In his last year of high school he was killed in a car accident.

When he was little I remember walking into the kitchen and seeing his head through the slats in the playpen. The front of his shirt was soaked with drool. Mom said he was cutting his first tooth but he seemed content, talking to himself as he turned the crank on his jack-in-the-box. I tried to sneak past but Bobby saw me and made a loud sound, extending his little arms straight up into the air like: touchdown! Which meant: Pick me up! I'm a sucker for that move. No possible way I could ignore it.

"Okay, hold your horses, hold your horses," I told him. Bending down, I grabbed him firmly under both armpits, and he made a happy gurgling sound, like a baby's idea of a song, as I lifted his soft little body into my arms. <u>He was a real good</u>

_baby, and a terrific brother. Not a day goes by that
I don't miss him._

You can see that at the end, I stand back from the immediate experience (picking up the baby). These final two sentences give me a chance to reflect on how my brother and his death fit into the larger fabric of my life.

This kind of reflection must be handled delicately. You don't want to hit the reader over the head with it: THIS IS IMPORTANT TO ME BECAUSE . . . Your reflection needs to whisper, not shout. I have learned to use a well-chosen detail or a line of dialogue to suggest the main theme, and trust that the reader will understand what I'm getting at.

Melody, an eighth grader, wrote the following piece when her sister Kathy went to college. Notice that Melody doesn't wait until the end to explore and explain why this event is important in her life. In almost every paragraph of Melody's piece we see and feel the larger impact of her sister's leaving:

As we entered this old dorm with all that Kathy thought she would need, I wished it were me. She would be on her own. She was going to live and go to school where there are lots of guys.

She was scared and excited. She would have a chance to be away from our parents and the responsibilities of family life.

She was leaving me with a room of my own. I was going to miss her but I didn't know what to say except: "If you need me I will always be here." And, of course: Good-bye.

I think it was hard for my parents because she is the first child to go away to school.

I was wondering who I'm going to talk to, now that she's not around. Kathy and I are so close. Would that change? I knew we could talk on the phone and she could still come home once in a while.

It was strange her not being there. It was like she was dead. There was nothing left to remind me of her. She had taken everything except her bed and empty bureau. I'm really going to miss her.

Her dream came true. She got to go away. She loves it there and finds it hard to leave. I envy her

*because she has such freedom, the kind I wish
I had.*

Important life transitions—a new baby, a marriage, a sibling going off to college—provide great
material for autobiographical writing because
they show the narrator grappling with an important life change. An older sister going off to college is a milestone in Melody's life that gives her a
chance to reflect on the past, the new present,
and her own future. This writing, like the example at the end of the previous chapter, has an honest, soul-searching quality that makes readers
want to find out more. In writing about any
important transition, the point is not so much the
specific thing (moving a sister into her first dorm
room at college) but rather why this was important to the narrator, what it meant for the narrator's life.

A Matter of Time

One of the trickiest issues you'll have to deal with involves the element of time. Handling time can be hard for any writer, but it's especially true with autobiography. That's because when you're writing about your life, long stretches of time are often involved. Not only that, but you find yourself writing about different kinds of time. In this chapter we'll look at three different kinds of time and how you can use them when you write a story.

• **TIME LEFT OUT.** When you write your life story, your tendency will be to start at the beginning, with your birth ("I was born in Plymouth, Massachusetts . . .") and continue with your earliest childhood years and so forth. I suggest you think hard before you settle on that approach. If you try to write about your life as a sequence, you'll be tempted to include lots of material (preschool, kindergarten, first-grade teacher, etc.) that won't necessarily be interesting to the reader.

"Do not write chronologically," advises Donald Murray, a friend and author. "Pick the most important moments and write about them in detail."

Murray's warning doesn't always hold true— there may be times when you want to write a sequential personal history—but it's worth considering before you start writing.

Consider how movies used to be made. In the old days, after they finished filming the actors, editors carefully looked at the film—miles and miles of it. They snipped out those stretches that were dull, flawed, or repetitive. There was an old saying: The more film that ends up on the floor— and gets thrown out—the better the final movie will be.

The same could be said about autobiographical writing: The more material that gets taken out (or never put in), the better the final piece of writing. Months, even years, can often be cut from your story without harming it. In fact, pruning those stretches of time will almost always strengthen your writing.

Let's say you're describing your relationship with your grandfather. One year you saw him at his birthday party, on September 1. The next time you saw him was on New Year's Eve. How do you get from September 1 to December 31? You don't have to include those events that happened in October, November, and December if they are not essential to your story. Instead, go straight to December 31. You don't need to write a fancy transition, either. Simply start a new paragraph: "The next time I saw my grandfather was on New Year's Eve . . ." The reader can easily make that jump in time.

Give yourself permission to do what those film-makers did. Cut! Snip! Delete! This may sound odd, but the most important time in your autobiography may be the "invisible time"—the birth-days, holidays, school days, and other stretches of time that you decide *not* to include in the writing.

• **PARTICULAR TIME.** Some people think you have to be super-smart in order to be a writer, but that's not true. The *last* thing most readers want is to have authors give a long-winded lecture on their "brilliant" ideas. Readers crave dramatic scenes the most—action, dialogue, and suspense. Effective scenes can take place in a relatively short period of time.

Adam's memoir "The Glove" (pages 33–35) provides a good example of a scene—something that happens at a particular moment in time. We hear the dialogue between Adam and his father. We feel as if we can see, touch, smell the old baseball glove. A scene like this isn't just a summary of what happened; rather, we feel like we're standing right there watching events unfold.

A scene showing a particular time can be fun to write, but writing a scene is harder than it looks. Let's look at a young writer trying to craft a scene about an experience he had with his grandfather.

"I want to show you something in the attic," my grandfather said.

I followed him up the narrow stairway. He took down a trunk that had stuff from when he was in the army. I saw his uniforms, belt, and hat. I read a newspaper from fifty years ago. He showed me two medals he got. But the most amazing thing was a gun he took from a dead soldier....

This could have been a longer scene, but the writer contained the important elements in two paragraphs with only one line of dialogue. The writer has given us only the seed of a scene. This scene involves one particular time, but it would be stronger if the writer had slowed down and given us an expanded version of exactly what was said when the boy and grandfather looked over those military artifacts.

Writer Barry Lane talks about "exploding a moment," swiveling the "writer's camera" around and describing a scene from different points of view. I think this is a helpful way of looking at writing scenes. You can pull the camera back to show the entire room full of people at your uncle's wedding, or zoom in to show the jagged scar on your brother's neck. When you explode a moment you use slow-motion, frame-by-frame details. This is a terrific technique for putting readers into the scene, making them part of the action.

• **HABITUAL TIME.** In *Marshfield Dreams* I wrote: "If we were good during church, if we didn't poke each other's eye out, my dad would stop at Leo's Bakery for the most delicious lemon-filled donuts in the world." When I wrote "dad would stop," I let the reader know that this was a ritual that didn't happen just once. Stopping at Leo's was something we did on many Sundays after we went to church.

When you're writing any kind of personal history you'll probably find yourself using habitual time, events, routines, or traditions that used to happen on a regular basis:

> After she ate lobster Grandma used to talk in her sleep.
>
> My sister and I always fought about who should get the biggest cookie.
>
> On the way to school we usually stopped to play by a stream near the Criders' house, and got our shoes all muddy.

Habitual time is an ingredient necessary to any autobiography. It can help you set a mood. You can use it to paint the landscape or background of what your life used to be like.

But be careful. When habitual time is used too often, there can be an uninteresting sameness about it. And because you're describing events that happened on a regular basis, habitual time tends to lack drama. The best autobiographical writing has a mix of habitual time and dramatic scenes. Habitual time is most useful when you want to set up one important event that took place. The following short memoir was written by Chris Wood, a fifth grader. Notice the moment when habitual time changes over to particular time.

My brother Jalen got all the privileges of being the oldest. He got new clothes. He got extra money for babysitting. He stayed up the latest. It wasn't fair.

Every year Dad would come into our bedroom, wake Jalen early in the morning when it was still dark, and take him duck hunting. I wanted to come, but Dad always said I was too young.

One night Dad came into our bedroom.

"Jalen!" he whispered. "Jalen!"

But Jalen was fast asleep. I sat up and blinked at my clock. 2:25 A.M.

"What is it?" I asked.

"Shooting stars!" Dad told me. "Millions of them. C'mon outside and look!"

I jumped out of bed and ran outside. Meteor showers! The next hour was the best of my life, standing on the wet grass next to Dad, watching neon-yellow lines streak across the night sky (I counted over a hundred), while my brother stayed in our bedroom, sleeping like a baby.

In some ways this sounds like a small moment (Chris watching a meteor shower with his father) but the first two paragraphs give us information to let us know that it's a big moment for Chris. Up until now his big brother has gotten most of the privileges in the family. Here we see Chris turning the tables on his brother and getting to spend special time with his father.

Dealing with the Hard Stuff

I wrote the following chapter for *Marshfield Dreams*, though it never appeared in the published book.

Blood Brothers

When I was a kid I had three best friends: Andy, Larry, Steve. Larry wanted the four of us to be blood brothers. He was always talking about it.

"All's you need is a little bubble of blood," he said. "We'll press our fingers together so the blood mixes. It's wicked simple."

We all agreed, and made a plan to do it first thing Saturday morning.

The next day after school Larry was helping his

cousin Owen tune up his car. Owen was a senior in high school. Larry and Owen had the car in the garage, the hood up, the engine running. The way I heard it, Owen was fiddling with the engine, when all of a sudden the flywheel spun off and cut Owen's head open. Blood gushed out everywhere. When Larry tried to stop the bleeding, he got his shirt and jeans coated with his cousin's blood.

Owen died.

Larry went to the funeral and we didn't see him for a couple days. His face was stone serious when he got on the school bus on Friday morning. I noticed that he was wearing a new pair of jeans and a clean white T-shirt.

Next day the four of us played in the woods just like we always did on Saturday morning. Larry never said another word about us being blood brothers. And nobody else mentioned it, either.

This piece includes some of the major themes of my childhood—close friends, secret understandings, and the edge of danger. Writing about the tragic death of a young person is hard, but it's infinitely harder when that young person is a member of your immediate family. Look at this piece by Vinnie, a fourth grader:

My Baby Brother

I had a baby brother. His name was Joey. He was born early, so he was very sick. He had to go to the hospital a couple of times. He was one year old when he died in the hospital. I was going to Sea Side Heights. I was in the car when he died. My mother didn't tell me until I came back. I cried. I was very sad. My brother Joey had a stuffed horse. He had given it to me. I cried. My stepmother made one big tear. I loved my little brother. I played with him. His first word was Mama. He had very bad heart problems, so he went to the hospital with a blue face. I always wanted him to get older so I could play with him.

Vinnie's memoir is short but unforgettable—the details, emotion, and honesty. I can't think of anything sadder than the death of a little brother. And I've been there: I watched my brother Bobby get killed in a car crash when he was seventeen.

Don't leave out the bad stuff when you write your life story. Our most awful experiences may be the most important because they are the ones that truly shape who we are. Along with all the fun and excitement, every life has its share of heartache, loss, pain, and suffering. Certain people get more than their share. Your family gets evicted from an apartment. Your grandmother dies. Your brand-new skateboard gets stolen out of your father's car. After your parents divorce, your mother remarries, but now you and your stepfather don't get along. These difficult situations are all worth writing about.

In order to write about very difficult experiences, you have to make the decision to break your silence. That first step—that you're going to include a difficult experience in your personal history—is crucial. The decision to write about a painful experience takes a great deal of courage.

But guts alone won't get it done. When you start writing, certain obstacles may appear. You might feel embarrassed or ashamed or disloyal. Let's say your mother hurt you in some way. You start writing about it, but you feel guilty because you realize that even though she hurt you, she loved you too.

There are no easy solutions to these obstacles. It's true that our most difficult experiences can be the catalyst for powerful writing. But you should write about them only if, and when, you're ready to do so. It may be too painful to write about certain events in your life immediately after they happen. Sometimes a certain amount of time must pass, often several years, before you're ready to take the plunge and write about them. After you finish the writing, you'll want to choose carefully whom you share it with.

There are special ways to write about very painful experiences. For example, you can change certain elements or characters in the story. This gives you more distance from the event and makes it less personal, which can help the words start flowing. Brooke, a fourth-grade student, was in a school where a kindergarten student died. When the school put up a memorial marker for the student, Brooke was moved to write about it. For the sake of her story, Brooke changed the girl into a butterfly. This gave Brooke some distance from the tragedy and freed her up to write about it.

The Butterfly

Once upon a time, about six years ago, there was a butterfly and her name was Shelby. But something was wrong. Shelby had cancer and was very sick. She went to kindergarten when she was five. But she died at home or the hospital. When she was only five she died.

Her mother, father, and brother were sad. I could not bear it, so I started to cry. Some people say that she is watching us because she sees that we care. If you see her just say her name. Then walk away, but she is still there following you.

Turn around and she will be gone. Turn back around and she will be there but as a kinder-gartener. She will be in class and sometimes at home. She's there like an angel in the wind, but beyond the sky. Mostly she is over the rainbow and that's what I believe.

Even if you don't believe, she will say "I will be there." But if you see her, she will be a big cloud of dust, but she is running quickly after you like a running cheetah. She's a kid and she's an angel. She might aim at you with a thank-you for caring. She would say, "My mom and dad should say thank you," and I would feel the same if I died when I was five. Gwin Oaks Elementary, the school that she went to, left a marker to show she went to the school. But that school misses her so much. They want her there.

I asked Brooke's teacher, Adam Crawley, what happened after she wrote this piece.

"Brooke shared the piece with the kindergarten class and the parents of the student who died, all of whom were so appreciative," Adam told me. "Students truly do have a powerful voice!"

One of the most remarkable pieces of writing I've ever read was written by a middle-school girl in New York City. She had gone through some very difficult years, including her parents' divorce and being abused by her father.

On September 5, I went to court. The judge decided that I wasn't going to live with any of my family for a while. They put me in a Coney Island Group Home. So far I have had four fights with other girls, but I'm coming along okay.

The title for what she had written was "My Half-Autobiography."

"It's kind of a sad story so far," I said. "But there's something hopeful, too."

She looked surprised. "What do you mean?"

"You titled it 'My Half-Autobiography,'" I pointed out. "That means you've got the other half of your life ahead of you. And that should be different."

"I hope so," she said, and managed a smile.

Interview with Kathi Appelt

Kathi Appelt is the author of *My Father's Summers: A Daughter's Memoir*. The book describes Kathi's childhood in the late 1960s and early 1970s when her father was in the military and frequently away. One day he returns home, but Kathi senses a new distance between the parents. She describes how her parents' marriage falls apart and how it affects the family. This powerful book is written as a series of very short chapters. Kathi has also written *Poems from Homeroom: A Writer's Place to Start; Kissing Tennessee: And Other Stories from the Stardust Dance;* and *Down Cut Shin Creek: The Pack Horse Librarians of Kentucky,* a nonfiction book coauthored by Jeanne Cannella Schmitzer.

Q: Your memoir, *My Father's Summers*, is full of tiny details—special cowboy boots, *My Friend Flicka* lunch box, etc. How did you remember all these details? Did it help to look at photographs?

A: I started writing the book about a year after my father died, so his loss was very fresh for me. In many ways, I felt like all my nerve endings were "raw," and that rawness made the memories more vivid somehow. It's hard to explain, but the details seemed to come flying at me, and it was actually the objects themselves that helped me recall the moments. As I wrote, I kept a running list of all these objects, the lunch box, the sponge that my stepmother used to wipe off the counter, the different items of apparel. I'd be writing about one thing, and while I wrote, something else would pop into my memory.

I didn't turn to the photographs until well into the writing. But the photos have been around for years. My grandmother kept them, and one of the things we did with her any time we visited was look through all her photographs. She was a great archivist. She even kept the rejected photos, the ones that ordinary people would throw away because they were blurred or everyone's eyes were closed. She loved them all. But she wasn't a careful archivist. She mixed all the photos up so that hardly any of them were chronological. She'd have a photo of my dad as a baby right next to a photo of my own son as a three-year-old next to a photo of her sister when she got married. Kind of a hodgepodge. And I think that's why they were so interesting to look at, because they were in such disarray.

As a writer, I love to find the extraordinary in ordinary details, especially objects. We associate ourselves with the objects that we collect or own or have to have, the things we carry with us, the stuff we live with. I'll never be able to dissociate my grandmother from her wooden salad bowl or my grandfather from his vodka. It's the common objects of our lives that tie us together. We recognize them immediately, have a clear vision of them right away, and so for the writer they become portals, really, to a whole array of sensations—sight, smell, taste, etc. The objects are endowed and thus invite us into the world of the writer, creating a union between writer and reader that is unmistakable and verifiable all at once.

Q: Some of your chapters are quite brief, as short as one line! How did you come up with the form of your book?

A: I have a close group of friends, four of us, who call ourselves The Poetry Girls. We've been gathering for years to drink beer, eat peanuts, and write poems. We're sort of like a book club in that we choose a book to use as our guide for writing, and for about three or four years now we've used Steve Kowit's book *In the Palm of Your Hand*. When we got to the section on prose poems, I felt I had discovered my own true form. I love the prose poem for the way it feels—it's dense, like prose, but because it's called a poem, the writer can take liberties with tense, point of view, etc. The blend of free verse with the solidity of prose felt right to me, especially for this particular book. So, it looks like prose, but doesn't have the true constraints of prose. It's looser. Freer.

Another thing I really liked about the form was the way it looked on the page, like a paragraph for the most part. And somehow that worked too. In other words, the content seemed to require something more substantial on the page than the shorter lines of a traditional poem. It was as if the line itself wanted to go all the way to the edge of the margin because that's where the material wanted to go. And I really didn't want all that open space that comes with a regular poem. White space has too much air, and I wanted these poems to feel grounded.

The "squareness" of the text also echoed the squareness of the photos, so that both the text and the photos resembled a kind of scrapbook. And in the end, I think our memories come to us in these small snapshots. Scraps.

The exception was the one-liners. In some cases, these could have been left at the bottom of the preceding poem. But I wanted the reader to have the breath of a page turn there. It could have been my experience as a picture-book writer that conjured this up. Who knows? I didn't want to use them often, but in the few places that I did use them, I wanted them to carry the weight of the whole page.

I also really wanted the book to be friendly. Part of the reason I wrote it was because I know so many kids are facing a similar situation—shared custody, stepfamilies, missing-ness—that I wanted the book to be something that they could see themselves in. But I also wanted them to see that they could write their own books like this. That you don't have to remember everything, just small details here and there, that the writing doesn't have to be long and drawn out, that it can be as simple as remembering your lunch box and the fact that every morning your mother packed something in it, and in doing so, therein lies a kind of grace. I wanted to show that love appears in the everydayness of our lives, like the sugar roses on a birthday cake, and the crab caught in a coffee can.

Q: Did you do much research (talking to your sisters about that time in your life, reading old newspapers, etc.) for this book?

A: I didn't do much research. I had to check a couple of dates. And there were a few things that I asked my sisters about. One of those was the incident where the boy next door to my grandmother shot my sister with the BB gun. I remembered it so clearly, but I couldn't remember how old we were. When I asked my sister about it, she hadn't recalled the incident in years, but once she was reminded, it came back to her as if it had just happened.

The interesting thing about bringing up these events with my sisters was how differently we saw some things. I would remember something one way, but they may have recalled it from a different perspective. I don't think this is unusual. Each of us approaches an event or an occurrence through our own lens of life, even when we're very close.

Q: You write about some painful topics—divorce, your father's drinking too much. How were you able to write negative things that might hurt the feelings of someone you love?

A: On the painful topics, I have always believed that pain can be turned over, at least somewhat, to the welcoming page. The page itself doesn't resist, doesn't judge, doesn't deny the pain given to it. It simply allows itself to be used. One of the fortunate things about my father was that in the last years of his life he did stop drinking. He was an avid member of Alcoholics Anonymous. So, he had come to grips with his own illness and had found some peace with me and my sisters, and we did with him, too. That was one of the great sorrows about his death. He had melanoma that was diagnosed on Thanksgiving of 1999, and he died right after Christmas that same year. He had been sober for almost six years. In so many ways, my sisters and I felt almost like the universe was playing this cruel joke on us—it seemed as if we had just gotten our father back when he was taken away again. But we are all three grateful for those six wonderful years when he really was our father again.

His alcoholism was at the root of everything— his failed marriages, his distances, all of it. But he survived that, and in the end, it was those years in the desert underneath that Arabian sun that took him.

I really didn't worry too much about hurting anyone in this book because unlike some memoirs, this one wasn't a reckoning or tale of revenge or anything like that. I tried to write it as clearly and simply as I could, without trying to paint anyone as an antagonist, or trying to place blame for my own misdeeds or addictions or whatnot. My stepmother was tormented, but she wasn't mean or evil or anything like that.

I think it's a survival story, true, and I hope that young readers can see that part of it.

Q: How much permission did you give yourself to "invent the truth" in your book?

A: I felt pretty free to write what I needed to write. Memory is always slippery, and while I worked hard to be exact and as true as possible to the events and people I wrote about, I'm sure that there are plenty of moments that could be called into question. And like I mentioned above, we each see these moments in our own particular ways. I will be the first to confess that whenever you call up a memory, the act of calling it up is to exaggerate its importance.

Q: How did your sisters react to this book?

A: My sisters love this book. And my mother does too. But one of the sweetest things that has come out of this has been the friends of my father who have contacted me, people I never met who have somehow found the book and have written to me. They've told me stories about my dad that I never knew or heard, mostly funny stories. Another thing that has surprised me has been the number of fathers who, like mine, left their families, and who have told me how moved they were by my story, and several of them said that it finally helped them see how their own daughters must have felt. I can't, of course, speak for their daughters because each of us has our own story, but I'm glad for these men to see themselves in the story of one daughter.

Final Words

You can't learn everything there is to know about any genre (kind) of writing in one fell swoop, if ever. It takes years of working at the craft. When it comes to autobiography, I know that I'm still learning. In various ways—through poems, fiction, essays, and memoirs—I've been writing and rewriting my life story for the past twenty years. And I'm not done yet. You might think that the publication of *Marshfield Dreams* would mark the end of my memoir writing for a while. But as soon as I finished that book I started thinking of important events that never made it into that book. There just might be a sequel in the works— additional stories, events, and influences. Or maybe I'll write an account of my teenage years. The more you write about your life, the more material you realize you have to draw upon.

If you look at the cross-section of a tree trunk you'll see rings, each one representing a year in that tree's life. We don't grow a new ring each year, but as you grow up you'll gain layers of wisdom and perspective. In the future you will be able to look back and reflect on the events in your life you're experiencing right now. You'll be able to appreciate new points of view. You'll make new discoveries about how certain things (your zany fifth-grade teacher, or that sudden move to California) affected your life.

It's an odd thing with this kind of writing. At the beginning of this book, I pointed out that you're the world's best expert on your life. But through this process you'll learn a great deal about yourself, too. When you write your life story you're always an explorer, forever arriving on the shore of yourself. Bon voyage!

Some Suggested Memoirs

Before you start writing, I strongly suggest you delve into some published autobiographies and memoirs. Read as many as you can. And don't forget that writers read differently from other people. Don't just read *what* it's about but also *how* the author put his or her life story together and made it engaging for readers.

PICTURE BOOKS AND POETRY

Been to Yesterdays: Poems of a Life by Lee
    Bennett Hopkins, illustrated by
    Charlene Rendeiro

My Rotten Redheaded Older Brother by Patricia
    Polacco

Neighborhood Odes by Gary Soto, illustrated
    by David Diaz; and *A Fire in My Hands* by
    Gary Soto

The Relatives Came by Cynthia Rylant,
    illustrated by Stephen Gammell; and
    When I Was Young in the Mountains by
    Cynthia Rylant, illustrated by Diane
    Goode

Tar Beach by Faith Ringgold

When Everybody Wore a Hat by William Steig

When I Was Nine and *I Meant to Tell You* by
    James Stevenson

Where I'm From by George Ella Lyons,
    photographs by Robert Hoskins

CHAPTER BOOKS FOR YOUNGER READERS

The Abracadabra Kid: A Writer's Life by Sid
    Fleischman

Boy: Tales of Childhood and *Going Solo* by
    Roald Dahl

But I'll Be Back Again by Cynthia Rylant

Childtimes: A Three-Generation Memoir by
Eloise Greenfield and Leslie Jones Little

Don't Tell the Girls: A Family Memoir by
Patricia Reilly Giff

A Girl from Yamhill: A Memoir by Beverly Cleary

Guts by Gary Paulsen

Guys Write for Guys Read, edited by Jon
Scieszka

*King of the Mild Frontier: An Ill-Advised
Autobiography* by Chris Crutcher

*Knots in My Yo-Yo String: The Autobiography of
a Kid* by Jerry Spinelli

Little By Little: A Writer's Education by Jean
Little

Looking Back: A Book of Memories by Lois Lowry.
"I would like to introduce you to this
book. It has no plot. It is about moments,
memories, fragments, falsehoods, and
fantasies. It is about things that happened,
which caused other things to happen, so
that eventually stories emerged."

Marshfield Dreams: When I Was a Kid by
Ralph Fletcher

The Moon and I by Betsy Byars

My Life in Dog Years by Gary Paulsen

When I Was Your Age: Original Stories About Growing Up, Volume One and Volume Two, edited by Amy Erlich

Winterdance: The Fine Madness of Running the Iditarod by Gary Paulsen

A Writer's Story: From Life to Fiction by Marion Dane Bauer

CHAPTER BOOKS FOR OLDER READERS

Bad Boy: A Memoir by Walter Dean Myers

Four Perfect Pebbles: A Holocaust Story by Lila Perl. A family tries to survive the Holocaust at Bergen-Belsen concentration camp.

Growing Up by Russell Baker

Hole in My Life by Jack Gantos

It's Not About the Bike: My Journey Back to Life by Lance Armstrong

Night by Elie Weisel

No Pretty Pictures: A Child of War by Anita Lobel

Of Beetles & Angels: A Boy's Remarkable Journey from a Refugee Camp to Harvard by Mawi Asgedom

Rocket Boys by Homer H. Hickam, Jr.

Small Steps: The Year I Got Polio by Peg Kehret. The author contracted polio in 1949 when she was twelve. Describes her seven-month ordeal: diagnosis, quarantine, paralysis, and slow recuperation.